LOVERS SHOULD NEVER QUARREL

★ ★ ★

Poems You're Going To Love!

George E. Samuels

iUniverse, Inc.
Bloomington

Lovers Should Never Quarrel
Poems You're Going To Love!

iUniverse books may be ordered through booksellers or by contacting:

iUniverse
1663 Liberty Drive
Bloomington, IN 47403
www.iuniverse.com
1-800-Authors (1-800-288-4677)

Because of the dynamic nature of the Internet, any web addresses or links contained in this book may have changed since publication and may no longer be valid. The views expressed in this work are solely those of the author and do not necessarily reflect the views of the publisher, and the publisher hereby disclaims any responsibility for them.

Any people depicted in stock imagery provided by Thinkstock are models, and such images are being used for illustrative purposes only.

Certain stock imagery © Thinkstock.

ISBN: 978-1-4759-1068-1 (sc)
ISBN: 978-1-4759-1069-8 (hc)
ISBN: 978-1-4759-1070-4 (e)

Library of Congress Control Number: 2012906185

Printed in the United States of America

iUniverse rev. date: 4/3/2012

TABLE OF CONTENTS

DEDICATION

This compilation of poems is dedicated to all the lovers' who love unconditionally and know it is better to give and happy to receive. To my lovely family with love!

INTRODUCTION

Love makes the world go around and many people go around the world seeking love and that unrequited partner to love and share their hearts. The poems reflect the seeker, seeking the lover but once received, they expect there to be peace and harmony but that isn't always the case because love is all the intangible we can give, whether we receive in-kind or not. Sometimes we don't get to express our love with some one who appreciates it or we don't always give our love to those who express their love toward us.

Some dream of love and romance and so I express this in the poems Desire, The Hopeful Romantic and turn up the heat with Butterfly dreams and Butterfly Kisses.

We remember great loves now and gone and poems such as Lost Love, A piece of Candy and Many Loves, makes us smile again.

Some people think love is the results of arguments and quarreling and sometimes fighting but that is not love that is aggression and should not be tolerated or liken to real love for example, a woman told me that if you are not quarreling and/or fighting with your loved one that is not love. I realized she was mistaken but not alone in that belief process. Sometimes we don't realize one should not quarrel, but one should endeavor to love, be happy, and hopefully not allow petty things to breakup a relationship. Luckily that is an individual experience and only you know what is truly in your heart.

Love is a purity that is beyond emotion that exists like a single thread amongst all of us and beyond that knows no bounds and asks for nothing for you to quarrel about. But few understand and appreciate love on that level. We still choose to share our love with all whether they are willing or able to share theirs. Some assume there is a cost associated with sharing their love and assume it's a cash, carry business, or receive a lot and give none or very little, while others are stars in one-act plays saying they love but showing the opposite. Hate will never be love just like sun will not be water.

A discourse in the subject will cover even the love that is sung about in love songs but I choose to write poetry that will take you on a trip and to a place on a familiar or distant shore. So I invite you to come along and enjoy remembering love is for everyone.

If you can't forgive yourself and then start loving anew don't argue about it (smile). Just cite a poem about it that is love. This excerpt from one of the poems within should move you to the starting gate, enjoy.

THE LOVING SONG

Being of one is the being of another
Leaving one
Only to be with another
Only smiles and laughter make you feel
You have what you have been after.
A very special Love
A touch of your lips warm waves, vibrations of breath
Kisses when you came
Kisses when you left playing that
Song forming a place of Love
A place of care, Loving can't be wrong
For loving is a Song.

Enjoy this poetry with love in your hearts and hopefully you will come away with love instead of quarrels. Can you give love if not, you will after reading this poetry. Can you receive love, you will, after reading the pages herein they will entice you to love first yourself than others freely.

BEGINNING

BLESSED ARE THE LOVERS

★ ★ ★

Blessed are the lovers
Loving their way home
To be loved in a certain way
The dust blows up
The mud sinks
The lovers think
Is that all there is
Love for loves sake
Whether they live together
Or get to eat the wedding cake
They sing,
They laugh for laughs sake
And they play for the high stakes
Love is the name
Love is the game
After love what remains
Is it gold?
Is silver there?
For them to spend
So does a diamond cut both ways?
Is there love in the night?
The same as the day
Can you breathe love?
Give love for loves sake
Or do you wish to get something
That you feel is at stake
But is it your love to take
Is a heart only a card game?
Or is love and the heart, really have,
The same name, or meaning
Or it is just some subtle feeling
Where is love when it is gone

Or is it forlorn
Only in thought
Or is it fondly sought
For selfish reasons
Or for sex in loves season
When the flowers bloom and the pollen is blown
Into your lover's nostril own
So it causes you to chase
Your lover from first base to home base
Saying it is in due season
And lovers are loving,
Or is it for lovers being lovers
Without any selfish meaning
And the love is for unconditional love
And there not be another reason.

WASHING

Washing
Cleaning
Dusting It off
Clearing the cobwebs away
Opening the window to a new day
Letting in the sun light
Letting out the fear and fright
I knew my heart was there
And the way to it however obscure was clear
For one to see
If it was truly me
And you could move in and check out the view
If you were really true
And showed how sincere
You were
And that you do truly care
And willing to stand up
And show to me how rare
Is your love
Clean, washed in the sea of purity
Ready to flow into my river
And comfort me with absolute clarity
So that I will appreciate this gem of rarity
And will cherish this and you
And likewise show you too my sincerity
As we bathe together for an eternity!

Begin Again

Begin again
See you when
See how to let go
And a new begin
You love crime
Some love grime
Why I don't care
None of this is a race
Jails full of convinced,
Participants that sin is the win
Have failed to prove their case
The agony on their face
Life drained, their life out of pace
With the rest of the race

Love is divine
Not fit for a life of crime
But to be convicted of love
Then you can rise up above
Out of the mire
Tempered in the fire
For all to admire
That you are changed
No longer a hater
No more the love of crime

Ready to make the climb
So subtle, so sublime
That you are the hero
This is your time
To show your heart
Is open again

You have let go of the sin
And where you have been
To be in a new place
And you can now see,
Me with my new face!

I WANT TO...........

I want to cry
I want to laugh
I want to holler
I want to be quiet
I want to be sad
I want to feel happy
I want to be angry
I want to be peaceful
I want to hate
I want to love
I want to hit
I want to stop the fighting
All of these things I want
But don't need
Today I plant the seed
To get rid of all the things I don't need
And focus on what the Soul feeds
To make me and you a better person
And lets forget the things I have done
So I can grow to play with others
And have fun
Knowing this is all that matters
Love, peace, happiness,
And helping others!

LEARNING

WHAT IS NEVER?

★ ★ ★

What is never?
Where is it located?
How do I reach it?
Is it a journey?
Long or short
Near or far away
In the hills
On the mountain tops
Never
Have you been there?
Which direction did you go?
Do you have a map?
Is it close to,
A place called Ever
Who lives there?
What is their business?
Should I ask these questions?
Never
Why, not too soon
Am I close?
Did you pack to ever get there?
Never
Why not
It's all in your mind
Never mind
As if ever
Was following you
Never seen it before
But I think I will
Head in another direction
To the land of Yes
I can be all I can be

Now and forever
Don't believe those
Who say you can't succeed
Your dream, your vision
They say never
You say whatever!

A GREAT WEIGH

If you put love and hate on a scale
Which would weigh heavier or lighter?
I think Love is lighter,
Hate is too heavy to carry around
So I traded it for love
Love is so easy it almost floats
And makes you light on your feet
Is the wave as great as the dust storm?
I don't know but the wave of love
Coursing thru the plains, doesn't kick up much of a storm
As the dust you hate to breathe somehow kicks it up
Sunshine's on the plain and lights up hearts everywhere
As those who hate the Light of the sun
Hide in the dark on a cloudy day as you see the blue sky
Or is it hidden like the love in your heart
You try to keep hidden even from yourself
French fries make a dish but the love bubbling up in you
Makes you itch for the same dish
Like the longing for another kiss sweet as honey
Just like bees that take the risk to pollinate the flowers
And make us believe it's worth the risk
Great is the dawn holding back the sea
But can't hold back the love trying to unfold
To reach a loved ones heart
Whether done shyly or bold
Greater is the history of what was
But not greater than the greatest love story ever told.

CAN YOU COMPARE

Elephants have big trunks
Lions have big paws
Tigers have big feet
Buffaloes have big butts
Deer big horns
Fools big wrongs
Eagles big wings
Haters' big hang-ups
Fighters' big lumps
Athletes take big jumps
Painters' big brushes for their art
And lovers have big hearts.

PART OF WHOSE LIFE???

Is love a part of our life
Is hate a part of another's' life
It's not a part of my life
My heart is not to be used as a tool
To play me for a song
To practice hate is wrong
To not give me your love
Is also wrong when all is said and done.

BREAK FROM IGNORANCE

I break from ignorance
Because it is not the way
To be when we are not ignorant
The act is up
The shield is drawn away from the door
The window is open
So like a bird we are to take our leave
Our flight from the way of those
Who will think we are ignorant

No more I say
Today is the day
We leave the ignorant behind
And look forward
To the way we are, intelligent, wise
And full of knowledge
Of who we are today
To be and the way
In which we are to gain
The flame of truth
Burning away the dross,
The gross, the Ignorance,
The break of a new day
We are free!

THE TRUTH WILL COME TO LIGHT

The truth will come to light
The lovers say
That is the lovers' way
I say I love you
You say I love you too
But do you really care
Should not be, if you dare
Are you really in love?
Do you care enough?
Are you ready to prove you're up to snuff?
Because love is not enough
Unless you care, when
Things get enough
When times seem low
I want your love to flow
When times are high
I don't want you to deny
That it is, I you love
Not the noise of the party
That gives you a shove
Or distraction from below or above
The truth will come to light
If you think you can leave me
And take flight
When I am not around
And others come to play
Just because I am the game for a day
Or I am out of sight
And you have to consider what's
Wrong or right
Because the mind is vast
Real love in the heart,

Must be strong enough to last
But real love is in the present
And in the past
As the future will unfold
And love is the story untold
As we learn to love each other
And grow old
A truth to be told
But if you really don't care
And just having fun on a dare
And you can survey the damage done
But then it is the finding out
The bill of goods I was sold
About, you really did care
Is only truth and lies
Glad its time
For, the truth to come to light.

THE LIFE OF SMILES

★ ★ ★

In the life of smiles
There is sadness
In the life of smiles
There is much rain
In the life of smiles
There is torment
In the life of smiles
There is pain
In the life of smiles
There is a sun that shines
In the life of smiles
There is a reality beyond the illusion
In the life of smiles
There is real happiness
In the life of smiles
There is a heart beating for someone else
To succeed not fail
In the life of smiles
There is a sound so sweet
We call it music
So intoxicating the ocean sways
In the life of smiles
Frowns turn to smiles
Melting ice turned into water then steam
In the life of smiles
Hope lives, dreams come true
And space defies gravity
In the life of smiles
We remember we are not alone
Except when we forget who we are
And our place amongst the stars
In the life of smiles

We keep on smiling, laughing
And know the heart melts,
The goal of our intentions in order
To refine our thoughts and emotions
So we can rise above the sky
To walk amongst the heavens
As angels watch us
Strive to be as they are!

NATURE CALLS

THE LOVE OF NATURE

The love of nature
Do we care?
Are we lonely without it?
Can it be we are in love?
For those who can love
Or is the problem we hate ourselves
Or is it natural for those who don't care
To hate the natural
Pay homage to the plastic
Invest in the chemical
At nature's expense
Or is it our lack of love
In our life and the prosperity
To hate ourselves our surroundings
Our hate training at the hands
Of leaders and siblings
That we have transformed
Our hate record to take for granted
Nature's love of us
And have mis-informed the universe
Of our intentions
To protect nature's ideals
Even as we make a mass appeal
But fortunately, some of us, our love
Has risen above like a phoenix
And are showing the reciprocal
Of nature's love
In all we do, and eat
And how we be so we can meet
And be understood that love
Everywhere occurring naturally
On the ground, in the water
Like the stars in the heavens
And as we love, nature will return
That love with a bountiful of love in turn.

In The Flower

How does the lotus flower,
Explain the sun
How does the sun explain,
The morn when it has come
And the day is done
As night has begun
Does the moon take up the late shift?
Is the moon a sacred gift?
Or is life just meant to coincide
As the sky acts as a guide
To show us the way that is best
Between east and west
Does rain escape to fill our cup
Or does it come to
Erase the dust
Roses smile in envy
As gorgeous girls walk by
Tipping their hats
As the flowers multiply
To cover everything
Including open pig stys
As contention begins
With fish on parade
Beautiful babies being made
The smell of incense
From the temple as the sunshine fades
The morning glory closes its eyes
And wears the mask of night
As it tries to hide
Crickets come out to play
Frogs on a paddy dance the night away
We realize if only for a day
That all is well with the world
And everyone has been paid!

Psychology of a Rose

Psychology of a Rose
What is it supposed to be?
Red, white, yellow, pink and purple
Colors of a rainbow
Given to women to represent
What is beauty?
What is gorgeous?
Why so beautiful
The women or the rose
They grow up
Budding at first
Ready to become so beautiful
When they are full-grown
From a baby
Watered and fed
That is how they are bred
Sunshine everyday
They blossom with each and every ray
On their face
We look, see and are pleased
Only to be surprised everyday
As they become more beautiful
In a day, tomorrow
I will see them and will be psyched
Their beauty is totally complete
The women, and the rose.

WATER

Drink a drink of water my dear
Let the water course through your veins
Then let it flow through your body
As it flows let it show you the way
The water flows through you like,
The river that flows through the Ganges
As the Ganges flows through you
Your mind reminds you of ancient Egypt
As the water empties into the Nile
Visions of Cleopatra appear
You feel like Imhotep
And you rise up inside
For the power of the ancients
Are inside of you,
The light in you sparkles
Off of the drops on your lips
As it dips across the Great Divide
You take another sip
A sip so great
Noah readies the Ark
Knowing it is coming
But not worried for it will just pass by
Knowledge flows into your arteries
As your heart is filled with vitality
And once again you remember
Moses parted the sea at the Supremes' request
You think I too will save the
People from all the dread
From the drought
And I will thirst no more
For I have seen what this all is for
And your mind tastes

A taste of clarity
Of water's utility
And you realize
You don't want to waste
Another drop
Pollute another river
For you have seen Niagara Falls
And bowed before Victoria Falls
As you row thru the Serengeti
The Plains of Georgia have nothing on you
And even though it's hot in ATL
You thirst no more
For the crystal blue water
Has entered into your Spring
As it seeks its own level
Calm and peaceful
Quiet is the calm
Before the storm but
For now the sword of great fuss
Has been laid to rest
And all you can think of
Is my thirst has been quenched
And I can take a rest!

LOVE WHEN LOVE HAS GONE

The gentle sweet flowing sea
Gently flowing seeking its level
Meeting at a point building
Swelling and rippling
Whipping to and fro
Gaining speed and momentum
Roaring,
Overtaking and delivering a powerful blow
Covering everything in its path
Knowing no boundaries
Warm or cold
Only to lift up its voluptuous body
And go
Leaving only a memory of love
When love has gone.

DESIRING

DESPERATELY SEEKING

Desperate is the night
Seeking day
Desperate is the rain
Trying to land on the plain
Desperate is the wound
Seeking the Band-Aid
To hide from the sun and the shade
Desperate is the wound
Trying to heal before it is found
To have happened
Desperate is the way we waste
Our time
And with junk food our taste
Desperately seeking ways
To be and save face
From all who try to make a case
That we are not up to par
Par boiled, chilled
And fired crispy to the bone
As we seek to believe we own
All that we have experienced
Or all we have known
But instead we desperately
Realize we only pay rent
For we own only our tears
Upon our bed
The laughter we use instead,
Of anger and lies
That we are systematically fed
To realize we are full
And need to realize the cock from the bull
Called "this is how it goes"

To something more fulfilling instead
Such as I love you - you love to do,
Be happy we met
And life is forever not the daily dread
And smile that desperately seeking Susan
Smiles that all is well instead!

WHY

Why you were before
Why not now
I came
I saw
I wanted
But you said no
Now you say yes
As I go
To never come again
I wonder why
You were before
I was there
You were here
You wanted to
I said no
You said not sure
I said I wanted more
You could of
But didn't
I know we
Were here before
But it seemed
It was a different day
Today it is another time
Tomorrow time will go
I want to know what to say
So I will just go
And you will ask
Why were you here?
As if you don't know
And I hope you were here
For me too, my dear!

DESIRE

Desire
A street car after that name
Without a care of the list
Of things that I desire
I want much
Expect to receive a lot
Want all I can get
But care about how
I want this and that
I want what I can have and
What I can't have
Because I care not
What is required
A desire is like a dream
A want is a need
Or so we think
We want all we can receive
But we must know that desire
Can ignite a fire
To accomplish what we want
And not provide what we only desire
Or need but guarantee us
More of what we require
We expect much
Sometimes receive little
Get upset when we don't get what we want
Not realizing it is only a desire
Wants are wants
Needs are the things we should desire
And be happy when we receive
What we require
Dreams and desires

Is all but a dream?
Not a requirement to be
But a need or a want
We insist, we require
I desire all
I want all
I need much less
I desire what I need
That is the best
I know much is required
If all my dreams were fulfilled
So I purify my desires
In the purification fires
And select the best for me
And dream of that desire
Desire what you need
And you best fire your desires
To burn up, the unnecessary desires.

TRAINS RUN IN BOTH DIRECTIONS

Trains run in both directions
I see you going the other way
Do you see me on the other train?
I am not going your way
Best I wish you were going my way
Today I see you again
And I wonder if you notice me
You look but you act like I am here
Or not but I know you see me
Our eyes meet going both ways
But why are we going into different directions
How come you are not on the same trip as me?
I can change trains
Can you change for me?
Tomorrow when I see you
I will be on your side of the platform
Waiting, hoping you are on the same train
As I board the train, I look for you
And don't see you
Where are you? I look
I wonder where you are
But you are not there as the doors close
I realize I am on the train
Going in the wrong direction
Disappointed I look out the window
And see you across the platform
Looking earnestly for something
I wonder what it is
And why are you on my platform
And I am on your train
Going in the other direction

I see your eyes catch mine
And you realize I am where,
You supposed to be
A smile lets me know
You were looking for me and I for you
And maybe tomorrow we
Will be in the same station
Same time, on the same train
Even though trains run in different directions!

WHERE ART THOU?

Where art thou my love?
Have life times and society kept you from me
Where art thou?
Who looks upon the brow of the world?
And sees me staring back
Have thou forgot me in my dilemma
Have you remembered me in your mind?
Has the past been given until thee?
So the present can't get away
And the future doth appear
In front of me
In front of us
Behind is the past
I look and there is
A glimpse of a memory
The mirror reflects us seeking us
Our now, our beginning
To no end
Where art thou tis my heart
That we have not seen
The rose appears
The clouds go away
To reveal a sunny day
Where lays the tiger and its cats
The bear in the woods
The elephant and its enclave
Covering and protecting your heart
Trying to not let me in
As the rain pierces old hates
To reveal a renewed heart
For your new mate

Has thou given me all thou heart
Or have thou sliced it up
And given me a piece
Only for me to remain parched and dry
Wanting more to eat
More than meat
Or have thou given up
The rainbow for my pot of gold
Overflowing with bountiful
Of drops of golden ecstasy
Meant only for you and me
Doth thou promise to
Give me all thy might
No matter what I do
When we are together wrong or right
As I give to you all of me
Morning, noon and night
So that we can go off
To the moon, then to the sun
And to new heights
Before all is said and done
Doth I thrill you in the moon
Or do we awake from
A night of love before the dawn!

I Saw You in A Far Away Place

In a far away place I saw you
As you came close I recognized you
From a long time ago
I waited for you to recognize me
But you didn't
I guess you reap what you sow
You cried for I had forgot then your name
And your face was not the same
But as I watched you closely
I could see you were playing the same game
Did we do that last dance before?
Had we tried to go through the same door?
But realized it was not going to happen
Since you were acting just like before
I tried to reason hoping
You had changed and there was more
For me to hang onto
Since I thought you had grown
But I realized you still
Had control issues of your own
Sometimes we think that things change
As things go out of range
But we have nothing to hang on to
Since only time can arrange
What needs to be a wound?
And they say time heals all wounds
Or is it that it heals all ruins
Tough to say who meets at the right time
Big times are tough
And the tough can't tell time
But couples mark time until they realize
They are not meeting at the right time.

THE HOPEFUL ROMANTIC

Wishing I was there
Wishing you were here
Where I could see
If you are to be
With me anyway
Not only for today
But for all eternity

I need you to be
Who I need
As I need you
You also need me

I wish as wishful thinking
As the thought of you leaving
Has me sinking
In my heart that
Another day we will be apart
But I am hopeful
You will not let this happen
And be grateful
That I am always with (thinking of) you
And no thing can come between us two

I romance the idea
That our love is rare
Even Sotheby's precious antiques
Can't compare
But hope springs from my heart
And my romantic ideas

Rise to the top and my joy appears
There are no tears
Even when you are gone
No losses to mourn
Just happiness amongst the forlorn
And your love is still here
After your perfume has gone
And I am still the hopeful romantic
Romancing, still alone
But hopeful you will come
With the coming dawn!

BUTTERFLY DREAMS

★ ★ ★

I flap my wings
And think I can fly
I fly to the heights
Where I alight on to the high place
Hoping to reach the Divine
I fly all over the world
To be with all the people
Who are thinking of me
As I flap my wings
I dream of dreams of fields of clover
Prosperity all over
I wish for the best
And know that I am at rest
When I alight on top of a flower
I dream the dreams of butterflies
Who have become the fliers
After they have grown up
And come through the mire
Best dreams are those without care
That you dream and hold dear
But dare to dream
When you know that you are there
Amongst the dream
Without a care
And you can fly to your desire
I love to dream
Of all that I desire
Reality is here
But the dreams are everywhere.

STATIC
(FRICTION)

WORDS
(DO THEY MEAN?)

★ ★ ★

Painful	painless
Wrong	right
Free	slave
Laugh	pain
Cry	happy
Know	don't
Realize	lately
Done	just started
Learn	use
Stuck	travel
Go	come
Same	change
Be	can
See	not
Want	give
Receive	go
Do	worry
Be you	be happy
Trust	giving
Love	won't
Jump	high
Walk	run
Don't	worry
Then	now
Go	return
Now	ok
Done	till now
So	enough
Going	away
The	time
Isn't	now
For	love

CRY FOR NO ONE, ITS ONLY ME

* * *

Cry for no one
Scream about nothing
Don't worry about something,
Be angry for what
Mad didn't solve it,
It's a crime
If you don't see it
It's a shame
If you don't feel it,
It gets better all the time
If it is stolen it is a crime,
Don't get hijacked
By those who
Missed and got sacked,
Believe it
If you see it,
It smells good
It's better than food,
All for you
If you accept
Given to others
If you decline
Beggars can be choosy,
Don't miss it
By being too busy,
Its better to give
Then receive,
It is better for it to come
Then for it to leave,
It will get you high
But you can't buy it,

In your mind
You will fly
Like a wave,
It over takes you
You can bask
In the sun
If you want to,
A lot is better
Than a little bit,
You can itch
It's meant for you
But others want it too
What could it be?
It's only me
My love!

PAIN PLEASE LEAVE ME

★ ★ ★

Oh pain
Where do you come from?
How did you get in here?
Who let you enter?
It is forbidden here
Go like the night
Don't come back in the day
I am not wanting you
I release you into your own cave
Run and go
Stay away
Go somewhere else and play
Act like you don't know me
And visit those who seek you
I do not
I want to forget
What I got
And where I met you
Go now don't dilly dally
For its time to escape
It's not for me
It's not my fate
Goodbye pain
Leave me, cleanse from me
Like the rain
And I will forget you
And block the door
So you won't come again
I don't care
Whatever for
You are free
To seek another
And forget you know me
And I will forget you and me!!!!

BLAME

Blame not the lover who comes in the night
Blame not the flavor even if its
Not the one that is right
Blame your self, if it's your plight
That to get what you want
You have to fight
Late is the mate who comes after you are gone
Early is the plain truth to tell
You why your lover is gone
See yourself in the morn
Clearly until darkness comes
But it can't stop the coming of the dawn
And all of your problems, see them gone
Life is but a free standing still
Waiting for you to move before it will
Busy is the bee making the honey
While you work hard to make money
But lax when it comes to creating harmony
Life is a chain on a linked fence
That keeps us all together
Whether it's loose or dense
We are one family in the past and present tense
But some see us separated
And not equal, and that is the suspense
Because they are alone in this world
Which makes no sense
So life can be beautiful
If you don't just live a piece of it
But live it full
With good intentions and it shall
Fulfill your every dream in a nutshell.

MISERY LOVES COMPANY

★ ★ ★

Misery loves company
Holler at the boss
Holler at what you hate
What has love got to do with it?
Love is a company
If you go to work
And practice love not hate
You hate to love your job

Misery loves company
But many hate what they do
Or the boss
But can't suffer the loss
Pay or be paid
The job can't fade away
Unless you retire
Or quit what you hate
Before it's too late
Because misery is a company
Of people that don't want you there
Or don't like you are here
But you are there because you care
But they don't care
If you love or hate
Misery is not supposed to be your fate
Find a company you love
A job you don't hate

For misery loves company
But again you need to find
Love for loves sake
Then it won't be any misery
And maybe you will love a new company.

HEART, LOVE OR NOT

★ ★ ★

Love or not
Tie the knot
But not with my heart
I say
You may
See me or not
That is why I am not
Seeing my heart
Love you
Love me
And see
If I care
Or dare
To love you back
I attack
Your sensibilities
I tie the heart
In a knot
And ask that you love me
Or not
But don't hide your heart
From me
Or you
I will love you too
If you trust that I am
And you
Are or not
Love is in the heart
I open
You open or close
Or not

But you can love with your heart
Or not
Love Me or
I will not
Love you Too
With all my heart!

WHO YOU HOLLERING AT

Who you hollering at
You
I love to holler at you
Why
You like me to holler at you
Who said?
You didn't holler back
Why
You said you love me
And
You have not stopped me
I would
But you can't hear me
Why
Because you keep hollering
What
Since you love to holler
And
I didn't want to separate you from your love
But
So when you are done
Huh
I realize you have had your fun
So
I am going to not listen anymore
Ok
And just provide you with something since your throat is sore
And
I am tired of this and heading for the door
So
You wont get to holler at me anymore
But
Still love you to the core, bye.

I Hit You Up

★ ★ ★

I hit you in the head with a stick
I try to get in my licks
You owe me
I owe you
You pay now
Or you will find
The payoff this time
But why the rose
Not the stick
I am loving you
Not trying to make you sick
A love tap for sure
Recipe for love and more
We can use the blame game
But I am not sore
For what I did and more
But love shows you for sure
That the rose is adorned
Above the law
Of the blame, the same game
You used (and the stick) to close the door
I use the rose to hit you
Using the greatest law
Love is better than hate
Obviously I have proven
I love you more!!

LOVE OF WAR

★ ★ ★

For the love of war
Like a one act play junkie
They say they love
And they do it for the love of money
But it is for their own sake
The trouble they make
Looking to upset all
Then complaints they make
About the other side
A witness to the drama
Of love and hate
They set out to make war and rape
They think this is love
No, this is hate
This is war for wars' sake
No good to rob loot and take
All that doesn't belong to them
But explain about their duty
To a nation who practices
And advocates war and hate
And don't actually drink
Tea for tea's sake
But hate in a bottle that
Sells like license plates
Because haters aren't born
They are trained to hate
And this type of training is all wrong
And love should be taught
Instead so they can hear
Love's melodic song
Instead of the warmongers horn
And peace can be more than

A dream or forgone conclusion
And we can put to rest this delusion
That peace makes war
And you need war to have peace
You been lied to because war only makes hate
And only sets a date for more (war)
And the value of peace is an open door
For those who care about more than their selves
And realize the truth of Peace and love is rare
For those who didn't have
The diamond of understanding
That love appears to be scarce
War is a pity and a waste of the military
But then, what else can they do,
So don't be this silly.

A Choice of Weapons

★ ★ ★

A choice of weapons
What will yours be?
What can you see?
The bat, an iron
Guns, knives
Love, or words
You can say
Will you talk jive?
What do you need to survive?
What is the reason for the gun?
It gives no love
Can you talk?
Think or be
Articulate
If you had a choice
Of weapons
What would you chose
My way, your way
Would you kill everyone?
Or would you save the day
You can swing a bat
Are you skinny or are you fat
Do you paint pictures?
Or do you collect signatures
From those who can't represent themselves
Or are you out only for yourself
Do you need to sing your song?
To let everyone know what is right or wrong
Or you plan to bomb them senseless
And you think it is smart
Not realizing it is nonsense
If you don't choose correctly

Because weapons of choice
Mean you can choose
Not to smoke or hate
Or drown yourself with booze
So you then can talk
But not be sober
And walk the talk

My weapons of choice
Is the pen
Or love when I can
But I can articulate
Just the same
With or without all the fame
And I don't need a gun
To have my kind of fun
You can love, laugh
And that will help
Because a joke is a joke
That you can make with the folks
Remember make love not war
I can choose,
To use my weapon of choice
Called standing up for all of us
When it isn't just fun
And can show love to all
Because I am like the sun
I will live to shine
And use my talents
As much as I can to
To be a loving example, for all Mankind.

HATERS GAME

★ ★ ★

Lovers' open
Haters close
Lovers listen
Haters hear
Lovers' express
Haters like chess
Create a moving target
So you can't get close
Lovers' shine
Haters see the sublime
Lovers reveal
Haters conceal
Their real intentions
I believe
Lovers feel each other
Haters conceal
And hide undercover
Lovers target the heart
Haters act like it's a lost art
But haters will learn hating is a pain
When you can love
Which is the higher aim
And what you really want
More sun less rain
More real less game
Hearts open no shame
So refrain from playing the haters game
Love everybody just the same!

WHAT'S LOVE DONE FOR US?

★ ★ ★

Love bought us together
And love broke us up
Love made us happy
Love made us fight
Love kept us together
Love pushed us apart
Love made me stay
Love made you leave
Love in our hearts was true
Love makes us lie
Love is all we have
Love is not enough
Love made me put up with your crap
Why love gets a bad rap
Love hid it
Love revealed it
Love is all we have
Our love is gone
Our love will return
But you will always remain the same
So I go
Because I am tired of this love game
Since nothing will change
So what's love got to do with it??

TEMPORARY AND FOREVER

Love is………………..
We came and saw
We have been seeking and wanting more
We can have all we want
That is why the carrot taunts
Pulling us closer
To what we desire
And tries to give us satisfaction
From all that we acquire
But we fool ourselves
That all we receive is only for ourselves
Not realizing we should share
For all is here only temporary
The breath and the air
Is always available
The rich and the poor
Even if they don't
Or can't afford the fare
But some want to own our very air
For the material things
It is all temporary
Like last nights' fling
Unlike love which is forever
Because the heart aches long after
We care about things we think matter
Love stays even after, we are gone
It is around during the night
And in the dawn (or morn)
Even when the building burns down
Forever love in the heart is still found
It surpasses the day
It surpasses all the anger

It surpasses all the pain
No matter what, it remains the same?
It is stronger than plastic
Biodegradable but rises from the ashes
Like a phoenix
Who has risen and dashes
To his loved one
From you, me and thru the masses
Forever is my love
Just like the sun, moon, and stars
Like a dove, love has forever risen above.

FALLING FOR WHAT

★ ★ ★

I keep on falling in love
Where are you?
Falling for what or who
Why don't you love me too?
I know you love you
But you can't take the mirror with you
See one on the other side
Are you looking for me?
I'm looking for you
I keep on falling for you
What should you do?
We want to see you
How you feel or
Are you just falling for whomever,
Appears in front of you
Your heart is cold
My heart is old
Your heart can be bought and sold
For what for who
Why can't you see?
I'm falling for you
If you dare to care
I want you to choose who you want
Not you, not me, just who is
In your heart that you see
Visualize my falling for
And know no matter what you do
I'm still going to keep falling for you
For love is kind and blind
And real love is no line
But like fruit on the vine
Like wine, is best when it's served on time.

THE PRICE

★ ★ ★

Argue for what
Fight for what
More glory
On some untold story
What is worth it?
To prove you have guts and glory
But no love
No love is loss
You got it wrong
Hate born out of love
No way only confusion
Is the course of hate
And the so-called liking your hate
To judge whether to love or not
How much to give
Like a slice of cake
Acting stingy so all of it you can take
For you giving up very little
While mates try to guess
What's up like some convoluted riddles
Or puzzle with pieces missing
No one to fill in the empty space
But let all that negativity go
So you can take love in hand
With your mate and pass through loves' gate
Just like it was meant to be, like fate.

LOVING

LOVE

★ ★ ★

What is love?
Is it a had?
Is it a want?
A need
Been there done that
I am
You could be
With me
And you're here now
Gone tomorrow
I love
So I breathe
I see
I can conceive
Love
Believe its love
Been there
Know this
It is everywhere
Yes gone now here
Again and again
Comes now and then
Only here when you feel it
No I think it is there
Closer than breath
All around
Up and down
And we breathe it
Consume it
It consumes us
Till we know it is
And was here

Hopefully we realize
It is still here
Or as we wonder
Where it has gone
Only to return unknown
Like the sailor from the sea
And my sweetheart coming
Just to be with me
Don't know why
Just we are both high
Don't know if it is
Love or a lie
Whatever it is!

LOVE IS

★ ★ ★

Love is
Never having to say
I am
I am that
Love is
Never having to pay
Love is
A traveler
That keeps on traveling
Never has to stop
On any day
Love is
Waiting for you wherever you go
You will see it and will know
It is here and there
Love is
Waiting for you to come and then go
Patient as a tiger waiting on its prey
The sun setting in the sunset
Love is
I am you
You are me
I know you
You know me
Love is
Given and received
Shared and smeared
All over me and you
Can't you see?
Love is
My love for you
Your love for you

Mixed in with all that I want and need
Because love is
The reminder
The remainder
It adds up
To all or none
Give me all or give me some
Love is
Unspeakable
Talked about
Whispered
And shouted in a moment of passion
Or chalked up to the latest fashion
But love is
Never hate
I love it but I hate it
Never happened
Only I love it
Or it loves me
Or I love it back
So to sum it up
Love is
I love you
I love you more!

OUR LOVE LIKE A FEATHER

Light is a feather
The test for our love
It floats, it glides
It chides on its decision
To be in my heart where it lays
Waiting for me to decide
Is it you
Or is it I
It is to be
As I float above the earth
Watching you watch me
Looking for what you need to see
Without all the fuss
Confusion and muss
From the clouds that dart in between
Like girls friends trying to see if you mean
Me and you
Or is there room for them too
But they don't know we are light,
As that feather
We rise above the noise
We stay together no matter what
And can keep our poise
Even in the midst of a storm
Until again it is calm
Because we rise at the slightest breath
Winds of change
Cold or flame
Snow on the mountain
Earthquakes in the sea
We still are calm as a midsummer's night breeze
And continue to float above all the trouble

Or noise from the rumble
And land alight
With peace in sight
And at the first sign of trouble
Wrapped in our love we take flight
At first light!

WEALTH OF LOVE

★ ★ ★

Wealth of love
All the same
Part of the game
I play
You try to say
It's not a game
Than why do you play me?

Just the same
I walk to see
If you are serious
But you play me
Then wonder why I get furious
At what you do
And try to

I say it is all fair
In the game
Of love
The business if you dare
I know you care
But you don't show it
It is all in the game
But I choose to play
Just the same
I prefer to keep my money and game
Away from the crowd
And love of the game
And dream that you will respect me
Just the same
Is my aim

And you can develop a new frame
Without going to a new low or level of shame
Only to laugh and say
Learn to play the game
Of love and fame
And wealth because its all a game.

MANY LOVES

Love of money
Love of fight
Love of might
Love of the gun
Love for none
Love for life
Love for strife
Love of others
Love great for another
Love of a wife
Love of wine
But not before its time
Love of nature
Love of things pure
Such as vegetables
Lack of love for unnecessary labels
Love now and in the past
Love should not be only for cash
Love of the sun
Love for the things given
And all things fun
Love for ambition
And all things driven
To victory
Love life's' journey
To show love is for everyone
When love's free flight has begun
And continues through until
Love's virtue has run its course
And all arc in love
And the Supremes'
Mighty task is finally done!

NOTE TO LOVE

★ ★ ★

Life turns
For the better
For the worse
You and me
Love
For loves sake
Make a love note
Beat the bush
Beat the wall
Search the stream
See where the love beams
Shines and strikes you
Is it in the heart?
Is it in the mind?
Or is love everywhere
My love is big
My love is huge
My love encompasses you
Does your love grow?
Where does it go?
Looking for love,
Is not the answer
It is in front of you
It is facing you
Who do you love?
Does love, love you?
My heart is full
Of love
Love you too
Can you love me?
When, where
Who, how

Big love
Small love
Incessantly flowing
Love all is so easy
Replace the fear
Replace the hate
Replace the mean
With the love stream
From me to you
Where is my love?
Or is it for you
Who loves?
Who hates?
Who hates to love?
Me you, All
We love and happy you love
We love you too
Love all
So they can see love
Love!

LOVE OR HAPPINESS?

* * *

Love or happiness
Both you dope
Can't have one
And call it the same
As love goes
So does happiness
It's a shame if
You love and are not happy
Because its part of the same game
Settle for both
Don't trade one for the other
Then try to lay blame
If one leaves then there goes the other
Then the only thing left is shame
That you didn't see it going
So you could of claimed it
As lost and found
And this time prepared you
For both not accepting less
The next time love comes around
Then, just be happy.

LOVE THOUGHTS

In the solitude of my mind
I express forth rising tides
Of my love for you as
The truth of my heart is
Pounding upon the surface
Of my mind in a gentle sincerity
Only expressed through you
Shining forth thru the annuals
Of time

My memory of you
Transmitted through space
Is my being by your side
If only to express my love
For you

When I thought of you
With such ease everything
Slid into place
Brushed embers remind me
Of an undergoing affection that is
Set aglow when I think of you

I feel
Less when you are not here
I feel
Better when I see you
I feel
Best when we are together

The rose of our life
Has just begun to blossom

And glow a bright
Judging your expression
You feel as I do
Without further ado
I love you

Hidden away in a
Secret place is a
Present wrapped up
All for you
My love is the key
Open up gently
Don't spill
Sip slow
For its all for you
Pressure sensitive news
Has just arrived
Let me be the first to deliver
The message

I love you.

RELATING

FEEL ME

★ ★ ★

Can I feel me?
Can I know me?
Can I know you?
Can I feel you?
Can you know I feel you?
Can you know you feel me?
Feel and tell me
What you feel
I will feel
But I will feel free
Do you?
What do you feel?
When you feel me
Or what do you feel when you see me
I feel you when I see you
I know what I feel
Do you?
Can you know?
Can you experience what I feel?
Can you see what I experience?
When I feel
I know, do you?
Can you tell me?
Articulate it for me
Sensitize me
My feelings
And I will,
Feel the vibrations of your thought
Thinking about me
Then we can feel free
To feel
To feel each other

So can you feel me?
Can I feel you?
Do you want to?
Will you try?
Do it and see
What I feel
When I feel free!

SPEAK

★ ★ ★

Speak
Talk to her
Talk to him
Listen to the sound
Did you hear?
Can you listen?
Do you want to?
I said nothing
But she heard me
I looked at him
He heard the words from my heart
He sought me out
Then said nothing
I spoke to her
But she just smiled
What did it mean?
Was it love?
Or was it just a smile
I say she loves me
He loves me not
I love him
She loves me not
What do we say to each other?
I can speak
I will talk
I will say what has to be said
He better tell me what I want to hear
I am listening
Can she hear me?
I do want to talk to her but
He is sending me winks
For what

What does it mean?
Is it love that taps on my shoulder?
Why won't he talk?
She should speak
I guess we love each other
Or maybe I should look for another
Who can speak!

LIKABLE

★ ★ ★

Is likable enough
Do we need to refine
Our thinking or keep it rough
Able to stay apart
Keep our love like a dart
Easily thrown
But not often shown
To be real
Kissing, playing, dating
Having fun but not for real
Likable, not showing any real zeal
For likable people is what most people set upon
So that life is simple just a whole lot of fun
Then all of a sudden real appears
Hearts speak and whisper a dare
Love is obscure but definitely in their aim
Shouldn't you want it?
Shouldn't you care?
Likable they say is enough
Then wonder why their life is oh so rough
But one stay they have to say enough is enough
And want love but have made a mistake
They settled for likable
And sacrificed love for likable sake
And the love of their life
Realizes they are all fake
As soon as love asks for a test
For life's' love sake
Likable(s) one day will walk away
And love will have passed by
For hope that love will come another day
And you will have learned that

Likable is not love
And lies are only for lie sake
True love is the only way
For the heart to say
I love you not just
To settle for likable
Like welfare, only small pay!

I/WE

★ ★ ★

There is I in me
There is I in we
There is all in we
There is we in I
I am the me in we
We can't be alone
We will be one
We will be two
We will be three
You and me
You, I and we
I can see who you are
I am, you are in me
Aren't we together?
Then lets say we
Knowing I am
You are within me
I am within you
So that I am that I am
Is who are we
We are I am that I am
Do we agree?

BOYFRIEND

He comes and goes
Knows me and I know him
We are together as friends
I trust him He trusts me
We are together
As boyfriend and girlfriend
But when I think he is my husband
He goes with another girlfriend
And I realize he is just a boyfriend!

GIRLFRIEND

★ ★ ★

Girlfriend
Safe and sound
With me in my arms
My girlfriend trusts me
Loves me, I am happy
She is happy
To be my girlfriend
We have a great relationship
But she is only a girlfriend
Ownership papers
Neither of us has
Even though one of us acts like it
We kiss and know the Intimate
Being boyfriend and girlfriend
We love each other
Where all is well when we are together
When all is not well we are with another
Because we are friends together
Not husband and wife
But more or less to each other
Until we make the decision
To be wife or husband
Or more than a boyfriend and girlfriend.

WIFE CALL

★ ★ ★

All is abundant with the wife
All is abundant with life
All is abundant with love in the heart
Love is abundant
Love is flowing
In and out
Wife is waiting
To see much
You rest worry not
Much is given
Much is enough
Bless the heart
Bless the wife
Bless the time
Life is offering
So you can see the.......
The life with the wife!

LOST LOVE

Lost love, gone
Where did it go?
Away, where?
My heart hurts
To know I lost Love
Some don't care
When asked
Some don't know
Where love has gone
To some it is missing
And don't know,
Love has come
Or where did it go
Some don't care that
It went and come
And don't want to know
Others lock the door
So they can't get
More of the same
Hurt, disappointment
Suffer, disillusionment

While others report
To them it is only a game
Love is selfish with its aim
Others play to win, or lose
While most chalk it up to only
Physical action
And wonder why they don't see it
Unless they came,
Love for some is stolen
And they didn't see the Thief

Who came in the night
And always leaves at first light
But love is so much more
Love is supposed to also be unselfish
Shared with friends and families of the same

Love when found is like a pearl
Larger than the world
Deeper than the sea
Only for the home of the brave of heart
And Noah's ark can't fill
But when shared can comfort all
Who open their hearts
Who can heed the call?
Where is your heart?
And don't chalk it up to art
Saying it is only in the heart of the beholder
But like a jewel must be found
Before you finish this round
And if you don't know where it is
Check the lost and found!!!

FOR ALL THOSE WOMEN

For all those women
Who didn't think their men cared
The nape of their neck
Their eyes wired open
Bright in the eyes
Sparkles like the sunshine
Laced with dew
The back so strong
We know they are right when they are wrong
But we want to make them happy
Hair straight or nappy
No one cares about the comb
Just the baby that came thru the womb
Looking for the Light
Waiting for love
Waiting for their eyes to open
To grasp at what is in their sight
Women are our mothers
Sisters and lovers
We need you to know
That we care, what about, you always,

But we have been the victims
Of things we reaped but didn't sow
We love all colors of your skin
And that is one way we know we are all kin
Akin to all that is reaped upon you
Including the whirlwind
And we support you where you are
Even if you didn't realize it any more
Blessed is the color of our family
Our community, for we are the soul of the rainbow

And together or apart
We are one with the All there is Thou Art
So don't get mad
Don't look sad
Don't take this life as a fad
And decide we are not a part
Of you, because we are
Your brothers, your lovers,
And your dad
For all women are who they are,
and need to be
So when you look into the mirrors
Know you are not alone
Look deeper and you will see me!

IT IS ON

★ ★ ★

It is on….
I came and saw you
The vibe was strong
The energy high
The words vibrated
Like strings from a violin
The reverberation sent me reeling
To a high place
My heart jumped into high gear
My hormones raced
I had to know who you were
We met eye to eye
The magnetism pulled us together
There was no opposite polls attract
It was like plates slamming your
Tits together to see inside
And I know it was on……
So I let it flow
No one could impede that kind
Of energy
Even a dam was not strong enough
And I knew this was about
What they write in romance novels
Oh yes it was on…..
Until you said something stupid
That made me forget all I had witnessed
By letting arrogance lead your step instead of
What we both witnessed in our hearts
So I shocked realized that,
You thought money could buy love
And you could take off your panties
And put on my big draws
No way honey
Yes it's on………

WISHING YOU WERE HERE

* * *

Wishing you were here
Holding me in your arms
Wishing you were here
Wishing you were here dear
It wasn't till you left
That I realized I care
Wishing you were here
Will not explain
The pain of when we last met
Those words I said
But they ill express
How I felt, what
My heart said

Wishing you were here
I only feel when,
We are apart
Talking to you I wasn't
Listening to my heart
But now its time to turn
Away from what I say
And listen to
What only my heart can
Bear to say
I am missing you
Wishing you were here
Wishing you were in my arms
Wishing you were here dear
But what can I do if
You won't listen to
My heart but mere words
That seems to keep us apart

Love, my heart speaks
Wanting to hold you so close
So dear
Far apart I can not bear
So I send this message
Not from our lips but
From my heart
Missing you and
Wishing you were here
Singing a similar song
Wishing you was here my dear.

LOVERS SHOULD NEVER QUARREL

Lovers should never quarrel
Why they make noise
Why holler and scream
Who jumps to the top?
Jumps for joy
Who fights the good fight?
With all their might
Just to prove a point
What is the point?
Lovers should never quarrel
Why fight
Why sing when happy
Why cry for big daddy
Poppa can't tell if you're happy
Mama can't say why she is crying
But both are happy
In love no matter when
Whether love is here now and then
And as it ended and when it began
At first sight
Or was it at first fight
For what they say
Some say for a great lay
Some believe in hate
Some think it is fate
No need to argue
No excuse to cause fright
To your partner, to your family
Then say I love you too much
There is no such,
Nonsense, but lovers shouldn't quarrel

Because quarreling only brings sorrow
And total regret come tomorrow
Then apologies and depression follows
And things said will be remembered
Today and many tomorrows
When another there is another seemingly
Small quarrel
So just be love
Give more love when there is a pending quarrel
And remember true love
Overrides any quarrel.

FREE AND FLYING

FEEL ASHAMED

★ ★ ★

Don't be ashamed about giving love
Be ashamed when holding back love
Be afraid when you have love and no one to give it to
Don't be afraid they won't except your love
Afraid to love
Be more afraid to hate then to love
Afraid you won't find love?
Be more afraid when you run from love
Don't be afraid they love you, too much
Be afraid you love them too little
And they know it
Be afraid of those who hate to love
Be not afraid of the love,
You give to those who do not reciprocate
Love is lovely when given
Received, cherished and not deceived
Love should not be hidden
But openly given
I am not ashamed of loving
I am ashamed of not giving love
Only wanting to receive
I am afraid of the game of love tag. . . .
I give when I get and not before, you are it!
Or I am giving love only to get
All I can to get you to do
What I want you to do
I am ashamed if you don't understand
Love is to be given away like a bad habit for a good reason
Give love all the time, it has no due season
So don't be ashamed to give
Love without a good reason!!

LOVES LABOR

Labor Camp
Stay, Struggle
Give in, Work
Pay, Lay
Rely Fight
Snuggle, One love
Open, Close
Stay away, Suffer
Give in, No regret
What to say, I love you
Each and everyday
At home, not there
And far away
To the ground
Sky is the limit
I give, you get
Far and beyond
Over the limit!

WORK FOR LOVE

Work for love
Work for life
Work and love is all right
But you should work to give love
With all your might
Scared to love
You should not fear
Love if you really care
Because love is given

Love like a blog
You can be smitten
And don't have to worry
Even if you marry
For love
And not for money
Because love is forever
And it's the greatest endeavor

Because the good work
Is for love's sake
And life is love
Not for hate
Especially for you and your mate
Learn this lesson early
And not wait too late
Labor for love for love's sake
And love what you do
And don't work for hate
Because love is what you want to do
Giving and receiving (from me to you)
Then from you to all and,
Then it will come back to you!

GET SOME KISSES

★ ★ ★

Am I dying?
Am I lying?
I am alive
I am living
I am loving
I am being
I am lighting
I am writing
I am guiding
I am trying
Am I flowing?
To new heights
I am happy
I am gliding
So I can see
What I am missing
So I can listen
To what is being said
And I am coming in for a landing
So I can get to the misses
So I can get some
Loving and kisses!

THINGS THAT ARE FREE IN LIFE

★ ★ ★

A smile
A touch
I love you so much
A kiss
A helping hand
Helping others if you can
A compliment
Good advice
When the timing is precise
A wink
A bite
Of food that helps the poor to be alright
Helping a child to understand
Helping a blind or old person across the street
If you can
A laugh
To help those who cry
To help them from a cry to a sigh
Only to laugh again
A hug
When they are so smug
Thinking life is a slug
A walk
A talk
When they don't want to be quiet
A prayer
For all those who can't
A way to show, you care
Things free of strife
Things that is free in life.

TELL THEM GO FLY A KITE

Is love a part of our life
Is hate a part of another's life
It's not a part of my life
My heart is not to be fooled
My love is not to be used as a tool
To play me for a song
To practice hate is wrong
To not give me your love,
When you love, is just wrong
I am happy to know my heart
Is full of song
Singing to your heart
Saying hello, not so long
So get with the program
Or otherwise I am gone
Stop vacillating about us
And old history,
Start now to write a new story
The past is the past
And we both can recreate a relationship
And build it to last
Or you can just be like others
And listen to members of the cast
Who want to make you act like an ass?
So they can laugh as your relationship,
Disappears just as fast
Because those who don't live with love
Hate to see you in love
So be careful when you meet these types
Don't listen to their gripes
And tell them you are a lover
And will love with all your might
And they can go fly a kite.

BUTTERFLY KISSES

★ ★ ★

Butterfly kisses
Wrapping lips around you
My arms to short to reach
All the way
I need your help
To be your love
Today

I am waiting for
Your lips
Open up the cocoon
Spread them wide
In unite---- me in your heart
For I am the one
You have sought
Searched for
Looked high and low

Thinking not
I am he
Hidden away
As my love for you grows
Inside
Like a dream
Coming true
I await your discovery
The winter of my moon

As the Sun appears
I am the me who is here
For you, now that you know
Don't you care?

That it is the time
For you to hear
My dreams, my dear
For you to become you
Full-grown

My love, your lips
Like a butterfly kiss
I only dream of you
When you are gone
Knowing you are full,
Of my love
And grown out there alone
Awaiting your return
To my home

Flap your wings
To fly back
And return to me
Fill me with your kisses
My butterfly
So I can sing
And soar
For the sun shines
And beckons your heart to my shore

Butterfly dreams
Are mine that it seems
I miss your butterfly kisses,
What is gone, will return again
Not in the winter of our dream
But again in the spring
I my love will not
Wait until you die
To tell you I love you
And you are all that I miss
When I walk alone
In the park
My heart jumps as

I see a butterfly
Soar onward
Towards the sun
Knowing it has flown
Its cocoon
For its love work is done

My butterfly dreams have
Turned into kisses
Many are one when
The day is gone
And all the butterflies have flown
I am now here alone
Inside of your cocoon
Warm and snug for another
Winter and spring
I see myself kissing you
In my butterfly dreams!

LOVE ON A TWO WAY STREET

One you walk down the other you lay down
One you stroll down one you float down
One you dream up one you make up
One you wish for one you ask for
One you live for one you try for
One you carry one you drop
One is up one is down
One gives and one gets
One believes and one you see
Invisible and untouched
Where one is temporary and contrary
To what you want-
     But
To the taste each one has its place
But whether you get either
I hope you get what you ask for
Because peace is peace is a piece
And love is definitely on a two way street.

FOR THE LOVE OF.......................

Birds are chasing each other into the sky
Don't you ever ask why?
Does the lovers ever chase each other?
Some say why the bother
Because life is a chase
Catch me if you can
Give me your love
Its not because, it is the wave of a fan
But a yearning in the heart and your hand
Birds chasing whom, who is running?
Who is fleeing?
Who wants to be with you?
Or is the chasee being chased
Or the chaser really the one running
Is that the real case?
Birds fleeing as if in a chase
Flying high above the earth
Maybe there is no chase
Just a case of heavenly elation
Because they are not stuck to the earth
And their desires are lofty for each other
To be with one another
And they are happy following each other.

TRAVERSING THE UNIVERSE

Traversing the universe
I ran into you
Before I saw you I knew you were looking for me
And when I looked inside all I could see
Were you and I, then I ran into you
And wondered why you went the other way
And did the things you do
Knowing you are better than that
And that your life is one,
That is supposed to be full of joy
Why did you turn away
When you saw me come your way
Trying to hide
As if I didn't see you that day
And I don't care what you do
Change is in the air
And now you know who you are
Stop doing what you do out of fear
You are not broke, you supposed to be rich
Think positive then it's an cinch
And know you are who you are
No matter where you go
True you reap what you sow
But new seeds doth a big tree grow
And you can change your fate
Because it is not too late
The universe calls to you
Where you flow
And life can be better
If you know who you supposed to be
Learn and grow into a teacher to help
Others who are low

Then you can stand up and help others
Traverse the Universe
Meet who they are to meet and know
And learn that their life can improve
Get into a better groove
And improve
So that when they change to the positive
They will learn you can reap what you sow.

SUN AND MOON TOGETHER

Who is ready for the sun?
Who can compete with the universe?
How do we come together?
Does the moon rise to meet the sun
Does the earth survive and pass,
The sun on a daily basis
Do energy flow the way of the fluids
Can time show us the moon's lover?
Can we see who is behind the sun?
Or the crimes committed in daylight
Or do we wait for nightfall to reveal
Our intentions toward each other
Does the moon's light reflect your love?
Or does the sun show its love to all
Even as night is called forth to cool off the day
And let the birds and bees sleep
From a torturous day making love to the flowers
Can a bright light hide in the closet
Or does your love hide in plain sight
Only to be discovered by strange bedfellows
Whose only idea is fun but not in the sun

Can you cut up and share what is meant for one person
And dole it out like chips on a salsa night
Or do you wait for the full cycle of the planet
To recognize the stars in your eyes
That reflects something larger than a whim
Can you alleviate the pain of suffering?
If you reveal your true feelings
Or does lies exemplify your anger on historical subject matter
That's lame and should be forgotten
Think, is this the end or the beginning

Is it the dawning of your new understanding?
That love is to be given, shared
And never put in the closet and forgotten
Like old rags after a shopping spree
Or is the dust in your eyes confused
With the evening coming
Or can you let the moon support her husband
And reflect the sun's light even though it is a supporting role
That everyone relies on but yet they shine on all of us
Together, no matter our plight.

NIGHTS OVER EGYPT

The sweet flowing ecstasy
Of my mind
When I meet your mind
Reminds me of the gentle sweet flow
Of the sea to and fro
The sweet white sand blowing
In my face
As I watch the gentle rushes of
The Nile in my heart
I know that you are mine
Come into my pyramid
And let loose your energy
When I meet the sphinx in you
I am flying high
And when we glide together
Across that beautiful blue sky
Nights over Egypt are nothing like
When your lips meet mine.

CANDY IS FOOD

FOR THE LOVE OF FOOD

★ ★ ★

For the love of food
What a pity
That we laugh ourselves so silly
At the idea of a gigantic food dish
Come on really
Food is for health
Food is for wealth
And without it there would be
A negative result
Yet some eat food and worship
It like a cult
For the love of you
One should eat food
For the good
Not only for the mood
Like a ring changing colors
With our every whim
Then this would help us to remain slim
And focus on love for loves sake
Two lovers a perfect relationship does make
And then for the love of the Soul
We begin to love others
Like we are all from the same one fold
And appreciate each of us
No matter the role
And then realize we should just
Worship light and love
In all we do from the heart to the Soul.

A PIECE OF CANDY

★ ★ ★

A piece of candy
He ate so fast
She liked chocolate
I liked the same
But peppermint was my favorite
She came I thought for me
But it was for the chocolate
I saw her eat the whole box
I asked, can I have some
She said, I gave you a piece
Be satisfied
I realized she shared it with others
I tried to understand
Candy is for everybody
But ours is supposed to be
Only for us
I didn't blame her
The times we lived in
No one cared for the other
But my candy I considered
To be sacred
I would not just give it away
To just anybody
I kept it safe just for her
When we saw each other
It was just a date
She loved to laugh
I cried for another piece
Of her candy
Good to the touch
Just enough for me
Not too much

Southern comfort is not only a drink
Candy may be sweet
But not too many calories
To cause me to deny myself
But she loves what I bring her
And saves just for her
And she has told me
She will stop the dancing
The shaking bumps and grind
And sharing her candy
With others
I await that day…
Is for what she says
Because candy is ok!

AFFECTION

There is but a endless sea
Of beauty that flows from the heart
The gentleness of the waves
Of affection rocking to and fro
Never failing to fill up our emptiness
Ceasing not continuing to flow on
Building, building wave upon ----wave
Enveloping us no matter
How hard we try to fight
And we drink not caring how........where
We bathe not caring who............when
But when we can
And no matter how hard we try
With all our might
That flow for some will come and go
Until we return to that endless sea
Of beauty called affection that
Flows from the heart.

MIX MASTER

Does the mix master mix love?
Or does he mix music
Does music groove?
And we dance
Or do we groove to the love
Can we hear the music?
Or do the tracks play what we love
Can we mix it up?
Such as love for hate
Hate for love
Or is it all in the mix
Don't shame us with your game
Like the pimp
Who thinks he has game
Or does he just love all the fame

Does the hater hate?
Or the hater love to hate
Is love even a factor
Does the trainer brush the horse's mane?
Or does he love to brush his own hair
Because he really cares

Is the melody playing to us?
Or does the harmony strike a chord
In our heart,
Or are we loving the noise it makes

Do we enjoy cake?
Or we just love to eat
Is love all we got?
And we are entwined

With love in all we do
Or is it a play about love
And are we endowed with the art
Is love given or is it sought
Do we give chase or
Give in and agree to play our part

I don't know, do you?
Or are the mix masters' lyrics playing on track
To educate what we think we lack
Music is in the soul
Whether we know it or not
I think that it is where love is
It is all around us (including what we do)
And that is a fact!

HEALING THOUGHTS

OVER WITH THE QUARRELS

What are you quarreling about?
What is all the noise?
Why aren't you full of poise?
I hear you scream
Like that you are anointed and thus deemed
What is your problem?
You seem to not be able to solve
Quit while you ahead
You are alive not dead
You can love just the same
If you will (would) stop playing those games

It's a shame
You can't see how high I aim
And you just want to go low
And settle for a life of so so
Mediocre is the name of your game
Settling because you don't seek fame
You argue too much
Come on get some guts
Stand up and be counted
For I am looking for a winner
Not some kind of a sinner

This is all ours for the taking
We can quarrel about less
Let us agree about more
Show me you can adore
All I have bought you and more,
For you to bask in
And let us out like kin
And love each other

Like this is the last day
On earth and we will be
Together forever and ever

Lovers should never quarrel
So no more quarrels
No more sorrows
Only much fun
You can lead or can follow
Because I am going up
Up to the mountaintop
Without a quarrel
And all you lovers' can follow!

THE MYSTERY

Mystery of love
Body so tight
Mind just right
Life so light
Finally we together all night
Fly to my heart
Be together when we are apart
What is the mystery?
It's just a category
You what, mad at me
Love you, love you not
What you want, what you got
Love for you, can you see it
Can we be, can you feel it
No, it is invisible
Can you show it?
Then I can prove it is real
Not just a mystery
Wondering where it is
Wondering where it went
Wondering is it at the end
Wondering if it is at the beginning
Not sure, do you want more
I know I love you to the core
Why do I?
I don't know but I do
That is the mystery!

How Do I Love Thee

★ ★ ★

How do I love thee?
Let me count the ways
A picture is a thousand words
A life a thousand moments
A love a thousand cares
Knowledge a thousand questions
Wisdom a thousand answers
The mind a thousand thoughts
Mistakes a thousand ways
No time in a thousand days
But there is only one way to say
I care in a thousand ways
I love you.

When My Heart Sings

★ ★ ★

When my heart sings
I think of you
Holler my name in your sleep
Dream I am here with you
Even though you, I can't keep
Why do I love you all the time?
When you are not here
Even though I want you to be here
I am here, there
On time, not late
For my dates
But time knows I am with you
Now and forever
My heart cries out for you
Love me, I say
We are to be together
No other way
Alive, dead
Awake, asleep
Peep at me
Know I am within you, so deep
You will be me
See me, become me
And with you, I am
Within, without
No doubt
I love you so I am
With you, I love you
You love me, be me,
I you love
It's you and me
So don't regret

That we are one
Together our hearts,
We will knit as one
Begin to melt
So we can return
I am yours
Be me today
I am with you your way
Just know I will come
If you will say,
Today we are one
Never more will we split
Our love, our life
We are together to the death!

HEART SOUNDS

★ ★ ★

Ringing in the ear so loud that I can't avoid
Wonder why we shout
So quiet the ear
I wonder why I hear it in my heart
How is the noise from the crowd?
That makes a noise so loud
So quiet
I am listening with all my might
Only to hear what is light
I am listening
Can you hear?
Or have you shut the door
So no noise can be heard
Or what your heart have said
To you, to all
So speak or listen
But open the door so you can hear
Yourself
Out loud
I can hear you
I am listening
Loud I am
Quiet are you
Do speak up
Out loud
I am listening
Are you?
Wonder why you cry, smile
Hearts speak out loud
Just open your ears and listen
You too will know what I am saying
To you, to all

Who will listen?
To my heart as it speaks
To you
Quiet, shhh
Listen, it is singing
You hear,
If not you need to talk from the heart
And then you will hear yourself
Listen carefully
So you can hear you
And your heart making sounds!

GIVING LOVE

Love is given when we know not
Love is expressed in so many ways
A kind thought from the heart
Avarice of concern, thought, even though unheard
A helping hand when needed
Love from the heart is expressed in so many ways
It is expressing love that we share
Together or apart, we give love to one another
Where it is known seen and unseen
Love is unseen permeating every level
It is not something that can be
Quantitatively measured
It can only be given and received
Allowed to flow
Rough or soft spoken
Witnessed or experienced
We can only know when
We receive it even though
To many they don't realize they are receiving it all the time
Giving it all the time
Love is love when pressed down
Shaken overflowing
No matter when we receive
In our expression of love
We learn about others and ourselves
We also learn about Divine Love
And compassion
Love is love and no one can change it
To anything else!

BE LOVE TO HEAL LOVE

★ ★ ★

Love you
Hate you
So what
I don't feel good
I love me
Hate you
Feel bad
Why I am sick
To be or not to be
Love, Hate
In the same place
I want love
You want hate
We can't be together
You hate
In the past
You hate the last…..
I love
I love that's my task
Completed
And in love
My love is strong
Your hate is strong
Why love, to do hate
When you can love
I am well
You sick
I love my health
I love, you can too
Be love
Release hate
And love wins

Health is better
Heart has changed
Why?
I love you
You love now, things can improve
You can be you
I can be me
We love, Heal us
Heal our relationship
All is well!!

OF LOVE OF SERVICE

★ ★ ★

We come to love
We come to serve
Giving is love
We love to serve
We love to receive
What a beautiful idea
No one else but He can conceive.

To love or not to love
That is the question
To give or not to give
That is the answer
And the water runneth
Or the water runneth not
Love is to serve.

Receiving, it flows to us
Filling, touching all sides
Overcoming, we accept it
Responding, we meet it and become one
That's the love, of service.

THIS IS OUR WORD

Give me love
Give me my love
Open your heart to me
I love you
Can't you see
Be my love and I will be your love
Love is in my heart
Give it to me
Give
I give it to you
Love is my way
War is not
I love you, this day
And every day, my love
And I hope you love me too
On the inside
Not just on the outside
Love, my word to you
This is our love
Our word!

THE LOVING SONG

★ ★ ★

Being of one is the being of another
Leaving one
Only to be with another
Only smiles and laughter make you feel
You have what you have been after.
A very special Love
A touch of your lips warm waves, vibrations of breath
Kisses when you came
Kisses when you left playing that
Song forming a place of Love
A place of care Loving can't be wrong
For loving is a Song.
Loving two in one
Heart playing our song
Take me to that dream
Take me to that place
Smiles dreams
Love touching
Feeling dreams
Light moonbeams
Kissing places to caress sweet dreams
Loving one
Loving one another.

LOVE'S HEALING POWER

Love's healing power
Flows like water
Healing, seeking
And filling all the holes
That is needed
To be filled
To be healed
To be corrected, changed
To show love's healing power
Inside, outside
And it knows no color
No one can stop it for long
For its power
Its stronger that the mighty river
Longer than the deep sea
Mightier than the warriors sword
Swifter than the bird in flight
And sharper than the point on the principals pen
Now and then
And it gives
Without asking
Who loses who wins
It is strong, and it is for the weak
And will conquer the war,
Hero and more
For it is tall and wide and equal on both sides
Of the world
And whispers to us all
To partake and fill
Our hearts, as hearts will
And share what we can't spend
Now or then

With those who cannot extend their hearts
And see that we all are a part
And can heal those in need
Of love
And to plant a seed
That can burst into a flower
And grow into
Life's healing elixir
Love is life's healing power!